INSTANT AUTHORITY

The Ultimate Strategy to Position Yourself as the Obvious Expert Allowing You to Eliminate Competition and Command High Prices

by Drew Laughlin, MBA

Copyright © 2019 Laughlin and Associates, LLC. ALL RIGHTS RESERVED. No part of this book may be reproduced or transmitted in any form whatsoever, electronic, or mechanical, including photocopying, recording, or by any informational storage or retrieval system without the expressed written, dated and signed permission from the author.

LIMITS OF LIABILITY / DISCLAIMER OF WARRANTY:

The author and publisher of this book have used their best efforts in preparing this material. The author and publisher make no representation or warranties with respect to the accuracy, applicability, fitness, or completeness of the contents of this program. They disclaim any warranties (expressed or implied), merchantability, or fitness for any particular purpose. The author and publisher shall in no event be held liable for any loss or other damages, including but not limited to special, incidental, consequential, or other damages. As always, the advice of a competent legal, tax, accounting or other professional should be sought.

Discover more about us by visiting:

https://CredibilityBook.com/

Note to Readers

Congratulations! You just took the first step in making sure you are known as the most credible person in your industry—the authoritative expert your prospects and customers will go to when they need your product or service.

By getting a copy of this book in your hands, you just unlocked all the secrets you need to create a Credibility Book of your own with very little time and money invested.

This book will tell you how easy it can be, what type of Credibility Books you can create, *and* how much of the process can even be taken care of for you while you're busy running your business.

Keep reading and find out how you too can tap into the powerful tool of Credibility Books, and watch the profits coming into your business soar!

Free Gift

As a way to thank you for investing in this book, I would like to give you a free gift.

The gift is a checklist you can use to guide you in writing and publishing your own Credibility Book in six weeks or less.

Imagine, for a second: in as little as six weeks you can be holding your very own print book with your name on it. How do you think that would make you feel? How impressed would your customers and prospects be?

To download your free gift, simply go to the webpage below and follow the instructions:

https://CredibilityBook.com/gift

About the Author

My name is Drew Laughlin, MBA, and I specialize in helping coaches, consultants, and professional service-based business owners publish a print book with their names on it in six weeks or less. This new book is a tool to help grow their business faster and more easily than ever by using our proven marketing strategies and systems.

A little bit about me.

I call myself a Business Results Specialist, because at the end of the day, it's all about results, right?

I am the author of the Amazon best-sellers *Expect Success*, *Client Getting P.L.A.N.* and hopefully the book you're reading now, *Instant Authority*.

As a former corporate leader in sales, marketing, and management, I have spent the last twenty-plus years helping consultants, coaches, and other entrepreneurs grow their businesses with proven offline and digital marketing strategies.

Splitting time between Omaha, NE, and Okoboji, IA, is something I love to do. There's nothing like being home for a Husker game and then driving up to the lake for some down time.

I am an avid golfer with a 10-handicap. I also volunteer as an assistant varsity high-school soccer coach— leading the keepers.

I'm a devoted husband to a rock-star wife and father to two amazing, ass-kicking kids.

But things aren't always roses and rainbows. I'm not perfect, and neither is my team. But I promise you one thing. Credibility Books are perfect for building instant authority and credibility and for being viewed as the go-to expert in your marketplace.

If that's something you want help with, then we're the people you need to talk to.

We not only invented Credibility Books—we wrote the book on them!

Praise for Drew and Credibility Books

I was recently a part of Drew's Credibility Book program. Jumping in, I wasn't sure what to expect, but Drew helped every step of the way! He demonstrated a very positive attitude throughout the process and helped me establish a series of goals in manageable pieces. If I had some questions or problems, Drew would take the initiative to help me over the obstacles and allow us to find a solution quickly. Overall this was a great experience, and Drew was there each step of the way.

—Paul Conant
author of *It All Starts with Marketing*

The Credibility Book program offered by Drew was everything as promised. Working with his team was amazing, and the response was fast. I got my book done faster than they had promised. The changes I had asked for were done quickly. Overall, I am pleased with the end product, and now I am working on getting the results from this great marketing tool!

—Randy Walden
author of *Learn How to Manage and Market Your Business Online Reputation*

Getting my book published with Drew was a great experience. He was helpful, professional, and courteous all the way through. Always willing to make any tweaks or major changes without the slightest bit of grumbling.

If you are thinking about getting a book published, I would definitely recommend you go to Drew.

—John McDonald
author of *How to Turn Your Website into a Customer Getting Machine*

Wow, I am so impressed with the final result of my book, *Protecting a Doctor's Digital Brand*! Drew was easy to work with. He was extremely receptive to my requests for changes and responded quickly whenever I had a question. There is no doubt I will be doing this again. I expect the book will provide me with a tremendous amount of authority working within the medical niche. Thanks, Drew!

—Joe Velez
author of *Protecting a Doctor's Digital Brand*

Table of Contents

Note to Readers iii
Free Gift iv
About the Author v
Praise for Drew and Credibility Books... vii
Part One: Positioning Yourself as the Authority 1
   READ THIS FIRST 3
   The #1 Authority Secret 5
   Who Can Benefit Most from this Book... 6
   The Authority in Author... 7
   Why Your Time Is Now.. 8
   Why You Should Listen to Me.. 8
Part Two: Your Secret to Success 11
   What Is a Credibility Book?... 13
   Why Credibility Books Are Superior to Traditional Books 16
   Five Unmatched Benefits of Credibility Books 20
   Who Should Write a Credibility Book?.. 22
   What Should a Credibility Book Be About? 23
   What Are the Different Types of Credibility Books? 24
   How to Use Credibility Books to Grow Your Business 31
Part Three: Your Blueprint to Success................................. 37
   What's the Best Publishing Process? 39
   Is There a Book-Writing Framework I Can Use? 41
   What is the Easiest & Fastest Way to Write a Credibility Book?.. 43
   What Size is Best for Credibility Books?...................................... 44
   How do I Create a Powerful Book Cover?.................................... 45
   Where Should I Publish My Credibility Book?............................ 47
   What Tools Do I Need to Create My Credibility Book? 48
   Do I Need an ISBN?... 49
   How Can I Make My Credibility Book a Best-Seller?.................. 50
Part Four: Making This Work for You................................. 51
   A Few Final Thoughts.. 53
   Seven Rookie Mistakes You MUST Avoid................................... 54
   Ten Common Myths... Busted! 59
   What Success Looks Like—A Case Study 65
   Do This Now.. 67
   Attend Our Free Webclass 69

Part One: Positioning Yourself as the Authority

READ THIS FIRST

Business is a dog-eat-dog world, and if you're not positioned in a way that allows you to be unique and stand out in a crowd, you might as well be wearing Milk-Bone underwear, because you're going to get eaten alive.

Ever heard the saying, "Perception is reality"?

Well, it's true. Whether we like it or not.

But I'd take it one step further and say: "Positioning beats perception every time."

Both positioning and perception are keys to being viewed as an expert, an authority on a topic. As the person people look to when they need their problems solved.

When you're not positioned well in your marketplace, you run the risk of being viewed like everyone else.

When you're not unique, you will be viewed as a commodity. And we all know what happens when something is a commodity, right? The only unique thing about it is the price.

Competing on price alone can be a death sentence to most businesses.

How different are you from your competitors? How unique are you compared to everyone else in the marketplace?

If your answers include things like, "We're locally owned," or, "We've been in business for twenty-five years," or,

"We're certified in _____," then you run the risk of being viewed as everyone else. As a commodity.

Things like those examples are *not* unique. Anyone can say them or at least something similar.

It's critical that you position yourself as a one-of-a-kind solutions provider.

And the cool thing is, you can accomplish this more easily and more quickly than you can possibly imagine.

At the end of the day, the real definition of insanity is doing the same thing over and over again expecting a different result.

Isn't it time to do something different?

Isn't it time to do something proven, yet simple, that can launch your business and income into levels you've always wanted but could never seem to achieve?

If you answered yes to those questions, good.

Let's keep going.

The #1 Authority Secret

Let me paint you a picture.

Imagine yourself talking to a prospective customer. They're asking questions about your business and the solutions you provide, and you say to them something like, "We literally wrote the book on that. In fact, here it is." Then you hand them a real-life print book with *your* name on it.

How do you think that person you will see you? As the trusted authority and expert? Of course.

Do you think they'll be predisposed to do business with you? Or at least to continue the conversation? Of course.

Do you think that this new position you have put yourself in will allow you to charge higher fees? Of course.

All of this can be accomplished by doing one simple thing...

Writing and publishing what's called a *Credibility Book*.

But don't worry. A Credibility Book is very different than a traditional book. We'll get into all the details in the following chapters, but for now, just know that Credibility Books are much shorter and easier to put together and can be completed in a matter of days or weeks.

Chances are you have all kinds of things running through your mind right now. "Writing a book" might not be on your to-do list. I get it.

All I ask is that you give me a few chapters to explain how this all works, and I promise by the end of this book you will be convinced one way or the other whether or not a Credibility Book is right for you.

Who Can Benefit Most from this Book

Before we get too deep into this, I want you to have a very clear understanding of exactly who this book is for.

If you're any of the following, this book is for you:

- Consultants (B2B)
- Coaches (business or life)
- Professional Service Providers (financial planner, accountant, real-estate agent, marketing agency—the list goes on!)
- Solopreneurs
- Business Owners

Basically, this book is for anyone who can benefit by handing someone in your target market a book with their name on it.

Think of it this way: people who use Credibility Books as part of their sales process have seen greater conversions, higher-priced sales, and longer customer lifetime values.

We use Credibility Books in very strategic ways to get the best results.

And I can't wait to share them with you in this book.

The Authority in Author

Odds are good that at some point, you've read a book to learn more about a subject or how to solve a problem you were having.

Maybe that subject was how to handle your finances, how to excel at a certain skill such as photography, or even just how to cook a better meal.

Whether or not you gained anything from that book is almost irrelevant to this discussion. What's not irrelevant is the reason you read the book in the first place.

You read that book because you thought the author was an authority on the subject. You trusted them enough to shell out your money and read what they had to say.

Have you ever met an author face-to-face? How did it feel? Almost like they're of star status. It's crazy right?

I remember a time when I was a sales manager in the corporate world, and the GM and I were planning some new sales training.

We both read a great book on a seven-step sales process that we thought our sales reps could benefit from.

We called the number on the back of the book to order a slew of books for our reps.

And what do you know—the author answered the phone!

You should have seen the look on my GM's face. He didn't know what to say at first, because he was shocked that the author of this book that we were going to use for our reps was actually on the phone.

Authors—for some reason—always gain immediate respect and authority. This is a great thing. And you and I can benefit from this phenomenon too.

If you're like more than 80 percent of people, you've thought about writing your own book at some point. As a business owner, you have a lot of knowledge and know-how that readers would benefit from.

And you'll benefit too, because you'll be forever known as the gal or guy who "wrote the book".

Why Your Time Is Now

Even though we're just getting started, I hope you already see what having a print book with your name on it can do for you.

That's why now is the right time for you to get your own book and position yourself as the go-to expert in your marketplace.

Let's separate you from all the other noise out there so you can increase your sales, raise your prices, and make the income you deserve.

Why You Should Listen to Me

In college when me and my friends would talk trash to each other, one of the things we would say—rather sarcastically—to prove we were right was, "I wrote the book on it!"

Even then I knew the value of a book without really knowing the value of a book.

Fast forward to me leaving my cushy corporate job after ten years, and I discovered the real value of a book. I started working as a certified trainer / sales rep for an author and speaker.

By far our most effective marketing strategy was getting the author's book in the hands of the decision-maker. When I succeeded in doing that, making the sale was the easiest thing ever.

Soon after I witnessed firsthand the true power of having a book with your name on it, I published my first of many books. And my life changed. Business got easier. People looked at me differently—with more admiration and respect and as the expert in my field.

I had so much fun publishing my own books and the benefits that came along with them I knew I had to help people do the same. That's when I decided to start helping others publish their own books.

And, boy, am I glad I did. Everyone I talked to wanted to publish a book, but no one knew the first thing about it or how to even get started.

Now my team and I focus every day on helping people publish their business-focused nonfiction books.

As a result, we have helped many coaches, consultants, real-estate agents, financial planners, therapists, and other professional service business owners create instant authority in their marketplaces and grow their businesses fast.

And it all starts by publishing your own Credibility Book.

We literally wrote the book on Credibility Books! We're the inventors of them, and we know all the ins and outs.

Read on to discover all the secrets of Credibility Books so you can see for yourself if publishing one is right for you and your business.

Or if you already know it's right for you, contact us at the webpage below:

https://CredibilityBook.com/talk

Part Two: Your Secret to Success

What Is a Credibility Book?

Let's start by getting very clear on exactly what Credibility Books are and why they are so much better than traditional books.

Credibility Books are one of the best resources for marketing, positioning, and conversion you have available to you. But what exactly are they?

A Credibility Book is a short book that is usually anywhere from twenty-four to seventy-five pages. While they can be longer, you generally don't want to surpass the one-hundred-page mark, because a long Credibility Book begins to lose its effectiveness.

Credibility Books also help the reader by solving a problem. This part is important. We've already established that you have a lot of information to share. But you don't want to share it all in one Credibility Book. These types of book focus on one problem and one solution. That's not overwhelming for readers. You're only giving them the information they need most.

Take this book for example. There's more than one way to build credibility, trust, and authority in your area of expertise. But I'm not going over all of them, am I? No, I am simply focusing on one way. It just happens to be the best way, too.

But your customers or readers aren't the only ones getting value out of a Credibility Book. You are too! After all, it's all right there in the name. Imagine handing someone a book with your name on the cover. That instantly builds credibility and authority. Usually business owners have to build a relationship and show customers time after time that they know their stuff, that they're the experts, before they begin to build any credibility with them. With a Credibility Book, you can do that in a matter of seconds. They really are that good.

This makes Credibility Books one of the best resources for any business owner. And they're especially great for business owners that don't yet command much credibility or authority in their industry.

Sometimes this happens with new businesses that haven't yet established themselves. Other times business owners talk to a lot of people or get a lot of hits on their website, but those prospects never seem to turn into clients. Some business owners just lack confidence, or they think of themselves as experts but don't know how to convey that to other people because they don't want to appear arrogant. They don't project their authority.

Whatever the reason is, business owners who do not yet have the credibility or authority they know they deserve will benefit from having their own Credibility Book.

If you are good at what you do but still find you're not making the potential profits you know are out there, you need a Credibility Book. If your current customers are always pleased with the amazing results you deliver, but you just don't have enough of those clients, you need a Credibility Book. If you are always looking to get ahead but still struggle with getting people to recognize your name and your brand, a Credibility Book can help solve your problem.

Once you have that credibility, potential customers and prospects are going to instantly trust you when you hand over a book with your name on it.

You'll be amazed once prospects start coming to you instead of you chasing them.

And the flood of referrals that starts flowing in without you having to ask for them.

At the end of the day, a Credibility Book will make you the obvious choice in the marketplace, no matter what your marketplace is.

Why Credibility Books Are Superior to Traditional Books

Hopefully you can already start to get a feel of why self-publishing a Credibility Book is a much better alternative than traditional publishing.

Just in case you're not clear, let me explain a few things.

First, it's nearly impossible to get a book deal with a traditional publisher. And if you do get one, you won't own the rights to your book. You also won't have total creative control, and it takes freaking forever to get published.

But most importantly you won't be able to market it in the ways that benefit you most.

Remember, you're publishing a Credibility Book to position yourself as the go-to expert in your area of specialization so that you can separate yourself from all other competition and command high prices.

While a traditional book will also accomplish that, it takes far too long, and you'll be losing out on thousands of dollars in revenue while you're waiting.

The Publishing World Has Changed

The publishing world is changing—Errr, I mean it's already changed.

The old model of spending months or even years writing a book just isn't worth it anymore. Going through a traditional publisher can take months—and oftentimes even years—before you're holding that print book in your hands.

In all, writing a traditional book and going the route of a traditional publisher can take up to five and ten years before you finally start realizing your original vision.

And even then, you may still not achieve your original goal. If your goal is to make money off the book or reach high levels of fame, the chances are good that you'll only end up very disappointed.

Of all the books that are written in the world, a very small fraction of them actually make money.

In addition to that, only a small fraction of books make best-seller lists. And even if you write yours in a way that is so engaging, interesting, and helpful that it does end up on a best-seller list, the chances are good that no one will ever know about it.

Best-selling authors just don't get the notoriety or attention they once did. And in the end, most people don't even realize what authors or books are on those lists—even well-known lists like the *New York Times* best-seller list.

Yes, it's true. Writing a book in the traditional sense likely won't get you any closer to the dreams. But there is still hope. And it comes in the form of *still* writing that book but writing it with a structure and format that is much easier, much quicker, and much more profitable for you.

It's a new world, and the more efficient structure of Credibility Books is the way to do it.

Do I Sacrifice Quality by Self-Publishing?

Because self-publishing can be easier, quicker, and cheaper than writing a traditional book, many people think they don't offer the same quality as professionally published books that come from publishing houses. But that's not true at all. The only real difference is that traditional books have to go through a gatekeeper first. And that has nothing to do with the quality of the actual book. And don't forget, all of the biggest publishers have had books that completely flopped. Going through a big publisher never guarantees the quality of a book itself.

Chances are if you've ordered a print book on Amazon, then you've purchased a self-published book. Not only did you probably not even realize it, but you couldn't tell the difference anyway, because the quality of self-publishing is world-class.

Who Wins in this New World?

People who serve others benefit most in this new world.

We're talking about entrepreneurs, consultants, coaches, and professional service businesses. Anyone who provides a useful product or service that solves a specific problem will win with a Credibility Book.

This includes people like marketing consultants, business coaches, lawyers, financial planners, real-estate agents— the list could go on and on.

Here's a simple comparison to help explain this further:

Old World (Traditional Publishing)	New World (Credibility Books)
⊗ Purpose is to try and make money from the book sales	✓ Purpose is to position yourself as the expert and make money on the backend
⊗ Fame and fortune to the masses	✓ Fame and fortune to your specific audience and market
⊗ 250+ grueling pages	✓ 24-75 pages
⊗ Takes months and months to write it	✓ Use proven frameworks to write your book fast
⊗ Must use a traditional publisher	✓ Self-publishing is quick and easy. Get your book in the marketplace in 6-weeks or less
⊗ Takes upwards of a year or longer to get published	
⊗ Must do all your own marketing	✓ No need for your own marketing
⊗ Publisher gets pissed if you don't sell lots of books or makes you buy 5,000 to put in your garage	✓ On-demand publishing means you save thousands

Five Unmatched Benefits of Credibility Books

As you can imagine, Credibility Books offer lots of benefits compared to traditionally published ones. Allow me to highlight the five most important ones.

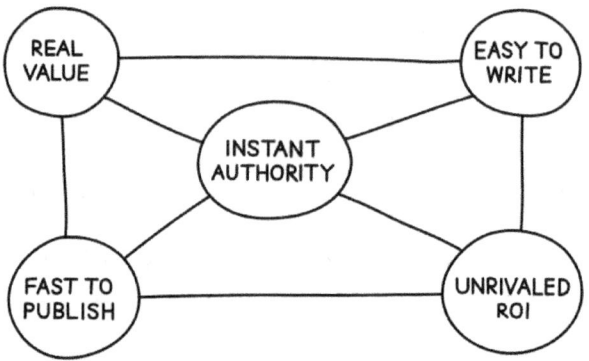

Instant Authority

Nothing creates instant authority and expert status like a book. And Credibility Books do it better than ever because they are not designed to be *New York Times* best-sellers. Instead Credibility Books are designed to give you the credibility, authority, and expert status you deserve through the simple act of handing someone your book. There is nothing quite like it.

Fast to Publish

Traditional publishing can take months or even years before you can get a print book in your hands. With self-publishing, you can get a print book in your hands in less than six weeks—and often times even sooner.

Unrivaled ROI

Traditional publishing can get extremely expensive. Most publishers will make you buy thousands of copies of your own book, costing you a lot of money. But by self-publishing—with an on-demand publisher—all the up-front costs are greatly reduced if not completely eliminated. And then you can invest in the books you need for just a couple bucks each. You can order as few as one at a time. Considering all the low-cost ways you can use your book to generate leads and customers, Credibility Books are by far one of the best assets that get the largest Return On Investment.

Provides Real Value to Your Customers

Unlike traditional books that are often filled with fluff and filler to make them appear to have more content, Credibility Books target one specific problem the reader is having and helps them bridge the gap from where they are now to actually solving that problem. Instead of having to go through all the filler, you'll bring value by giving them only the good stuff.

Easy to Write

Credibility Books are much easier to write than traditional books. With Credibility Books, you can have your content written in as little as one to five days. Why so little time? Because instead of providing a comprehensive book, you focus on one specific topic and answer questions your audience is asking in their heads.

Who Should Write a Credibility Book?

As we mentioned before, Credibility Books are perfect for consultants, coaches, entrepreneurs, business owners, and other independent professionals.

> In short, anyone who solves a major life or business problem will benefit from a Credibility Book.

Are you already successful at what you do but want to take your business to new levels? Then a Credibility Book is right for you.

If you're someone who is viewed as an expert in your field—or want to be viewed as an expert—you will benefit greatly from having your very own print book.

Basically, if you think you could benefit by handing someone in your target market a book with your name on it that positions you as the expert... this is for you.

What Should a Credibility Book Be About?

A Credibility Book is specific to one problem your target market faces, and it's focused on actually providing people value to help solve that problem.

And it contains *no* fluff.

Unlike traditional publishers who want you to have a minimum of 250 pages—which, let's be honest, most of that is fluff and useless information—a Credibility Book can be as short as twenty-four pages and done in a matter of weeks.

One of the major mindset shifts most of our clients have to go through is resisting the urge to solve all the problems in one book.

What we do is show them how it benefits the reader when you focus on just one problem and one solution.

In turn, this helps you too, because you can stay laser-focused on that and not worry about all the stuff that doesn't matter.

Often, the best Credibility Book simply answers the most common questions you get asked all the time about your product, service, and solution.

We'll talk more about that in the next chapter.

What Are the Different Types of Credibility Books?

Four common types of Credibility Books have proven to be the most effective for positioning, conversion, and marketing. Each one has its own purpose, and all you have to do is determine which one makes the most sense for you and your business. The purpose of each book, and some tips to remember when writing them, are described in this chapter.

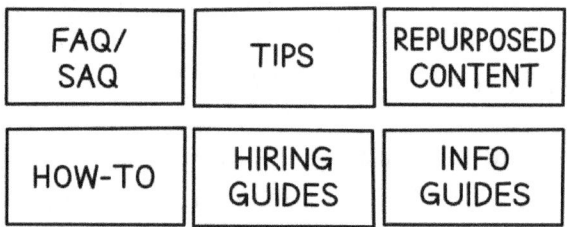

FAQ/SAQ Books [Most Recommended]

Every business owner gets asked the same questions over and over again. These aren't questions like, "What time are you open?". Rather, these questions relate directly to your products or services. Lawn care specialists may get asked time and time again how often customers should water their lawns. Marketing consultants may get asked over and over again how much online advertising costs. And home contractors may continuously get asked how long a bathroom renovation should take.

These are frequently asked questions, and to answer them, an FAQ Credibility Book can be a great resource.

Inside these books, customers will get answers to the most common questions they probably already have. And you, as the business owner, will be able to save time by not having to repeat yourself over and over again. And you'll be building your credibility at the same time.

In addition, you're the expert, and you know the answers that customers need, but they don't always know to ask the right questions in order to get those answers. It's a case of they don't know what they don't know. The customer with lawn care needs may not understand their lawn should be cut to certain lengths in order for it to grow lush and green. The business owner may not understand all the various online platforms to advertise on that best fit her business. And the homeowner may not know there are certain things they can do before renovation work begins to make the process easier and faster for them and the contractor. Those types of questions are called Should Ask Questions, or SAQs.

For these reasons, an FAQ/SAQ Credibility Book is one that we recommend to most of our clients.

These types of books are effective because you're able to build your voice as the authority in the industry. The reader will feel like you're inside their head answering the questions they have plus the ones they didn't even know they had.

I bet you didn't realize the book you're reading now is an example of an FAQ/SAQ Credibility Book. Pretty cool though, right?

Tips Books

These are just what they sound like. A book of tips can be useful to show your customers that you really know your industry. Not only do you know things that anyone can research and learn, but you know the insider tips that only a real expert would be able to understand. A tips book can really make you an authority, because people assume insider tips are accumulated by those who have been in the business for a really long time. You have the experience to understand what problems may come up and tips on how to solve them. Or, maybe there's a certain way other people in your industry approach certain tasks, but you have tips that can make it even easier and more efficient.

Think about the ever-popular cooking shows. Sure, anyone can Google a recipe that they want to make—but that's not why people watch those shows. They most often watch them to get insider tips from professional and celebrity chefs who have been in the business for a long time. They want to learn what the professionals know to make cooking easier and quicker. That's why those shows are such successes.

And the same can be said for professionals in any industry. When you've been in the business for a long time, you know things that can't be Googled. You have the tips your clients need to make their lives easier and more convenient. And a book of tips can include all those ideas.

Tips books don't have to include just tips, though. They can also include obstacles, common roadblocks, and mistakes to avoid. These too, are "tips," because pointing them out gives people an insider look at what usually trips others up and tells them how to avoid making those same errors.

A book full of tips and mistakes to avoid is typically the easiest to write. And they still provide a huge value to your customers. Plus, they can be a really easy read too, which your prospects will also appreciate.

Repurposed Content Book

Chances are you already have a lot of great content relating to your business and industry, whether these are articles on your website or blog posts that just didn't get the attention you were hoping for. Maybe you've created a whole list of YouTube videos trying to give your customers the information they need, but they just didn't get the views you had envisioned.

All of this content can be repurposed and placed into a Credibility Book. It's important to remember though, that Credibility Books focus on one problem and one solution. If you have a lot of content covering a number of different topics and solutions, you'll want to collect all the related content on just one topic and make one Credibility Book.

While business owners may not find these kinds of books as exciting to write as a tips book or an FAQ/SAQ book, these books still provide a great value to anyone that reads them. No one will know that this is content you've already created, and it will likely be content they've never seen before. They'll still get a lot of value out of it.

And a book full of repurposed content can provide great value to you, too. All these books need is a little tweaking of the content to help it all flow together in an organized fashion. This can make creating your Credibility Book even easier and get it done much faster. If you have a lot of topics to cover, you can create several Credibility Books in just a couple of months and be able to hand them out whenever someone has a question related to that specific topic or whenever you find a new prospect. You'll have a huge variety of Credibility Books to give them.

How-To Books

How-to books, and how-to content in general, are one of the mainstays in publishing. You can give prospects and clients a book that outlines how to do something, step-by-step.

Let's use a marketing consultant as the example. A consultant can put together a book outlining, step-by-step, how to use email automation to help systematize their marketing efforts. The book would go through each step of the process from beginning to end. This provides huge value to customers and prospects, because you're actually showing them how to do what you do. You're giving them the inside secrets.

But, why would anyone do that? Why would you just freely give that information away for people to do everything on their own, instead of hiring you? This is the number one fear of business owners when creating a how-to Credibility Book. But it is an unfounded one. People never take all the secrets and embark on the project themselves. Why? Because they don't have the time or the energy to do it.

If they did, they could learn most things with just a little bit of research. By spending some time on search engines, people can get all the information they need and do whatever they need themselves. But they have other things going on. They have their own jobs, their own families, and their own hobbies. They don't want to invest the time doing it themselves when they can hire a professional to do it for them.

You may be asking, why then would they even want this book in the first place? At the beginning, they may think they want to do it themselves. But when they start reading and see that its more cumbersome and difficult than what they thought, they'll want to hire someone to do it for them. And they'll want someone who knows how.

Hiring Guides or Info Guides

Another great type of Credibility Book is what we call Hiring Guides or Info Guides.

These types of books simply cover the most important things someone should know *before* they hire a person or company in that industry.

For the most part, those important things will pretty much be the same for most businesses in the same industry. But when you're the one who publishes the book, not only are you immediately viewed as the expert, you can also add in content that positions you better than your competition.

For example, a financial planner can publish a book titled, "Everything You Must Know Before Hiring a Financial Planner." The book will outline various things the reader should know before making a decision. The financial planner will cover these items, but at the end of the explanation they can describe why they're better than anyone else.

This structure is truly a win-win.

The reader wins because they're getting useful information to help them make a good buying decision.

The author wins because not only are they positioned well; they are more likely to earn that reader's business because they're the one who wrote the book.

How to Use Credibility Books to Grow Your Business

We help our clients grow their revenues by using proven marketing strategies specifically designed around their Credibility Books.

To go over them all is beyond the scope of this book. But I do want to explain a few critical elements to using Credibility Books successfully when it comes to marketing.

Let's start with how customers make buying decisions.

The Customer Buying Line

I created a framework called "The Customer Buying Line™" to illustrate how customers actually make buying decisions.

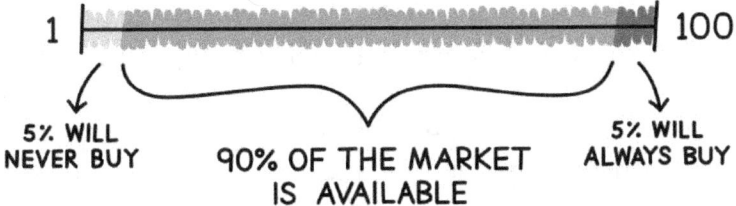

The far-left side of the buying line starts at one. These are people that will never buy from you. They may have a brother-in-law in the business, or they're already satisfied with their current provider. In fact, let's say that group makes up 5 percent of the market—the people who will never buy from you.

On the far-right side is the number 100. These are people who will do business with you no matter what. Happy customers or people who need your solution and yours is the first one they see. Let's say that the market consists of 5 percent of these people.

Unfortunately, 99 percent of the way businesses typically market their products and services is for the 5 percent on the right-side of the Customer Buying Line. No wonder most marketing fails.

Combine the 5 percent who never will and the 5 percent who always will, and that's a total of 10 percent of people we don't need to spend time or money focusing on.

But what do we do with the rest of them? The 90 percent?

Often times those people simply need more information to make a buying decision. They need to be moved down the Customer Buying Line toward that 100 number.

They may make a decision way before they hit that number. We don't know what their buying number is.

Our job is to provide them with education and information to help them make the best buying decision for them. As we do that, they move down the buying line closer and closer to a purchasing decision with the person or company they feel is the expert.

During that time, we build trust, credibility, and authority.

And the best part? It can all be accomplished by simply handing them our book.

They can move from 6 to 100 that fast.

I could write an entire book on the Customer Buying Line™ (and probably will someday). But hopefully I've shown you how it works, why it's important, and how using a Credibility Book will help move your prospect down the buying line and closer to making a decision to do business with you.

Bypass the Gatekeeper

Often times when there is a business we want to work with—that perfect business—it's tough to get in front of the decision-maker. Rarely can you get through to them by cold- calling. Chances are you're faced with leaving countless messages with their assistant—the gatekeeper—that never get returned. You've tried to set up a meeting with them time and time again, only to be repeatedly told that their schedule is too busy and they have no time to meet with you.

This is a very common problem. But it's one that can be easily overcome with a Credibility Book. This is one area in which you can really make these books work for you. All you have to do is send a copy of your Credibility Book directly to the decision-maker. While the bigwigs of the world may not always get their messages, and they certainly don't always respond to them, they always get their mail. And they will always look through their mail.

By sending your book to that one person who's been impossible to get ahold of, you've just bypassed the gatekeeper and gotten your foot in the door.

Simply by having a Credibility Book, you've gotten their attention, and you might just turn that huge prospect into a huge customer.

IMPORTANT: this is one of the most effective strategies we employ. It works like a charm.

Online Lead Generation

We've been talking this whole time about print books. As we should be. That is the main focus of this book. Later on, I'll explain how easy it is to create a print book and ebook at the same time. That is important because offering something of value such as a report or a ebook on your website in order to generate leads, while not a new strategy, is still very, very effective. People see the item of value you're offering, they enter their name and contact information into an opt-in form, and they get the item of value.

In this case, that item of value is your Credibility Book or ebook. In turn, you get a lead that you can then follow up with, providing them with additional value, asking them if they've read the book and if they have any questions, and telling them how you can help. You already have the book, so why not use it to its full potential?

Your Ultimate Business Card

All business owners have met a potential prospect at some point. And often, when the owner meets these leads, they end up talking to them for quite some time about a problem the prospect is having. This can involve an in-depth conversation in which the business owner tries to tell the prospect exactly how they can help. To be honest, this can take a lot of time. Much of the time, that conversation itself doesn't help convert the prospect into a paying customer. Instead, it ends with the business owner giving the prospect a business card and asking them to call—which the prospect may or may not do, depending on how the conversation went.

But imagine if the next time you meet a prospect that has a problem you know you can solve; you hand them your very own book instead of a business card. Your Ultimate Business Card, if you will. You'll save yourself time, and you'll also build your credibility with the prospect so much more than any one conversation could, because an entire book can cover much more ground than you can talking to someone for just a few minutes.

While there's a lot we can do for you to get your Credibility Book out to those who need it most, there's also a lot you can do too. There are so many ways you can use your Credibility Book to increase your business. We've highlighted just a few in this chapter, but there's more where that came from. Feel free to contact us if you'd like more information. (See the end of this book for contact details.)

Part Three: Your Blueprint to Success

What's the Best Publishing Process?

A lot goes into writing a book. Even though a Credibility Book is far easier and much faster to write than a traditional book, it still takes work.

The good news is we have a simple yet proven framework you can follow to go from an idea to a print book in your hands in six weeks or less.

Here's a high-level overview of each phase of the process now.

The Credibility Book Publishing Framework

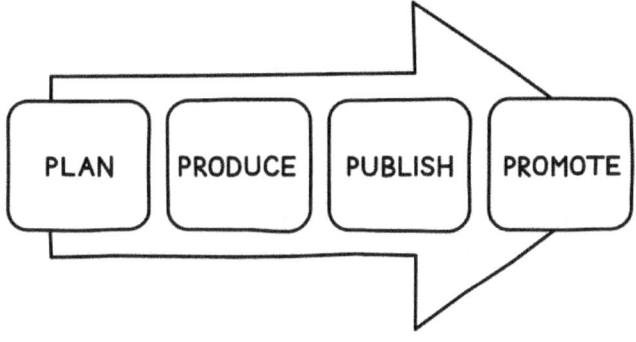

PLAN

The Plan phase is just that. You plan out the book you're going to write. For example, if you decide to write an FAQ/SAQ book, then you start listing all the common questions you get on a regular basis. After that, you list out all the questions someone in your market *should* be asking.

Another part of the planning phase is to identify what free gift you'll offer in your book. This is to get people to go to your website and opt in to your email list. This is proven to be very effective, so don't ignore it.

PRODUCE

This is the phase where you actually start writing the content. Or recording the content and getting it transcribed. You will also create your book cover.

PUBLISH

This phase is where you actually publish your print book through the self-publishing platform of your choosing. (We share our recommendation later on in this book.)

PROMOTE

This is the phase where—you guessed it—you start promoting your book. Whether you use some of the promotional ideas described in this book or more of our advanced ones, this is where the rubber meets the road, and you start becoming the authority in your marketplace.

Of course, there's more to each phase than what's listed here, but as you can see, it's a simple process that works, and it's one you should follow.

Is There a Book-Writing Framework I Can Use?

A Credibility Book is much different than a traditional book, and so are the ways we outline and write them.

Ultimately, we structure it in a way that makes it look similar to a traditional book, but our focus is a much different.

We focus on four main areas.

And it's no coincidence that they are the same things that are most important to people who will end up reading your Credibility Book.

The four areas cover the four ways people learn and absorb information. To have the greatest impact, you need to cover all four.

The book-writing framework breaks down like this:

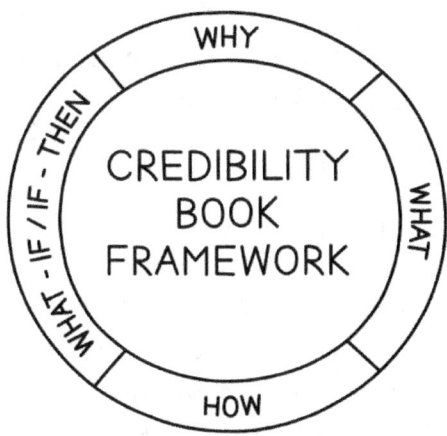

These four sections fit inside the overall structure of the book but make up 80–90 percent of the entire contents of it.

Here's a brief explanation of each of these four areas:

The Why

The topics in this area emphasize *why* solving the problem you address is important. Granted, most of the time people will know why, but you need to "twist the knife" on their pain to make sure they'll want to solve it sooner rather than later.

The What

This area covers *what* your solution is, at a high level. It explains what people need to do to solve their problem.

The How

This area covers *how* you go about solving their problem. Again, you don't go into great detail about it, but you give the reader enough information so that they know you're the expert and in turn will hire you to fix it for them.

The What-If / If-Then

This area covers various things that may come up in the reader's mind and what they should do about it to still solve their problem. This area should also include rookie mistakes to avoid and bust any myths that will prevent them from moving forward.

What is the Easiest & Fastest Way to Write a Credibility Book?

Full disclosure: writing your Credibility Book is actually pretty easy.

This is because you're already the expert in your business, and you already know the content.

You know the things that your prospects want to know about before they make a buying decision.

Want me to prove it to you?

In every business, there is a series of the most common questions that people ask you over and over again. You can list out all of these questions and answer them. That is the focus of our FAQ/SAQ Credibility Book framework, which makes for an extremely powerful Credibility Book in and of itself.

Of course, there's a little more to it, but I'm sure you can see how easy it is to simply answer questions you're already getting all the time.

It does not have to be any harder than that. In fact, we recommend that you do *not* make it any harder than that.

What Size is Best for Credibility Books?

The best size for a Credibility Book is 6 x 9. It's a very common size that most people use.

The minimum number of pages you need is twenty-four and using a 6 x 9 size book allows you to reach that without too much trouble.

It's small enough that even with twenty-four to seventy-five pages, it still "feels" like a larger book.

Another common size is 5.5 x 8.25. This is a smaller size, but it's one that is still pretty common and good for reading.

Amazon's KDP publishing program—the one that we use and recommend—offers both of these sizes and more.

How do I Create a Powerful Book Cover?

Most people are not graphic designers—nor should they try to be just to save a buck.

It's best to hire a professional to do it for you.

But that doesn't mean you give up creative control.

The process we suggest to our clients is to take an hour and look at a slew of books and pick and choose some that you like that resonate with you.

That way you can give that list of books to your graphic designer—along with other pertinent book details like title, sub-title, colors, what it's about, and so forth—and they will be able to design something for you that you'll love.

You can also use a service like 99 Designs and have several graphic designers compete to create your perfect book cover. The cool thing about this is they all create the design first and you get to pick the best one.

For clients that work with us, we offer a ton of sample book covers that people can choose from. However, we also create covers from scratch, because we believe in making sure your cover is unique and stands out just like the content inside it.

While the topic of book covers could be an entire book on its own, the most important elements you should be aware of are to keep your covers simple yet bold, and remember that less is more.

Front Cover:

- Title: We love one- to three-word titles that stand out and can be displayed in a large font. It makes it easier to read and looks great. Notice the title of this book: INSTANT AUTHORITY.
- Subtitle: Your subtitle should be very descriptive and benefit laden. And if it makes sense, you can also include something to avoid that your audience hates.
- Author Name: Unlike the ego-centric authors of the world, we do not recommend that your name be larger than the title. Remember, it's about your audience and not you.
- Image: If it makes sense and you have an image that strongly relates to your book then use it. But it should be clear and simple—nothing complicated. And no stock photos.

Back Cover:

- Testimonial: We recommend putting a customer testimonial at the top for social proof.
- Headline: Adding a strong headline to get attention is always a good thing. It leads to...
- Summary: This should be a very short summary with five to seven bullet points.
- About the Author with Picture: This is a short summary area about you with a professional picture.
- Offer: We highly recommend putting an offer for something free by including your website URL.

Where Should I Publish My Credibility Book?

We use, and recommend to *all* of our clients, Amazon's KDP—Kindle Direct Publishing—program.

Publishing on KDP allows you to immediately get listed on Amazon, but it also gives you the ability to publish your book on Kindle as well.

Remember, we're not looking to sell thousands of our Credibility Books. That's not why we're publishing them. But getting listed on Amazon and Kindle boosts our credibility even more.

Another huge benefit to using KDP is it's *free*.

It costs nothing to become a published author. And it isn't just ebooks. KDP provides a printing service called "Print On-Demand," where your book is printed when someone orders it, and you do not have to buy a garage full of books like you would with a traditional publisher. In fact, you can buy as few as one book at a time.

Lastly, KDP is very inexpensive for you as the author too. The cost per book is ridiculously low compared to other publishers. The low costs make it so you can use them with a bunch of different marketing strategies that otherwise would be too expensive with a traditional publisher.

What Tools Do I Need to Create My Credibility Book?

One of the great things about self-publishing is that you don't need a lot of tools or software or programs.

All you need is:

- A word-processing program – like Microsoft Word, Pages, or Google Docs
- A graphic designer for the book cover
- An account at Amazon KDP

That's pretty much it as far as tools go.

Do I Need an ISBN?

An ISBN is an International Standard Book Number, and all books have one. So do you need to get one? No.

When you use Amazon KDP, they will assign an ISBN to your book. It will show them as the publisher. But not to worry. You still keep all rights to your book and content.

However, if you want your own ISBN, you can invest in one. At the time of this writing, the cost is $125.

You will also need to form a publishing company if you choose to use your own ISBN number.

That reason alone is why we typically recommend you do not buy your own ISBN and just left Amazon KDP assign one to you.

Check out the details for this book on Amazon. You'll see they are the publisher. ☺

How Can I Make My Credibility Book a Best-Seller?

Hopefully I've stressed to you enough by now that making money from book sales alone is *not* the purpose of a Credibility Book.

Nor is the fame of being a world-renowned best-selling author.

Rather, our purpose is to position us as the go-to experts in our areas of expertise. And that's exactly what a Credibility Book does.

With that being said, we do have a proven system and process that helps Credibility Book authors reach best-seller status for the Kindle version of their book.

However, that is a completely separate topic we cover with our book coaching and marketing clients. Once you write your Credibility Book and you want to get the Kindle version to best-seller status, let us know. We'll be happy to help you.

Part Four: Making This Work for You

A Few Final Thoughts

Congratulations! You've made it to the final section!

Since you've made it this far, clearly that means you are truly interested in publishing your own Credibility Book. You understand the benefits it can bring to your business.

But before you take the next step, I want to touch on a few more very important things to ensure everything is covered and to answer as many questions as possible.

In this section, I reveal seven critical mistakes a lot of people make when starting out. I don't want you to make these.

I also look at the top ten myths people have in their heads that are simply not true. I enjoy squashing them for you.

Lastly, I have a case study from one of our many successful Credibility Book publishers. Greg's story is the perfect example of not only how easy it is to publish your own Credibility Book but how you can use it to grow your revenues in a major way.

Keep reading to get the goods.

Seven Rookie Mistakes You MUST Avoid

Writing a Credibility Book will be very beneficial to you and your business. But some common mistakes crop up along the way. By avoiding these mistakes, you won't waste the time, money, or effort that you might if you fall into one of them. Watch out for these slip-ups and know how to sidestep them, and your Credibility Book will be everything you imagined it would be.

Over-complicating the process

Literally every day someone sends me a message with something like, "I don't think this will work for me." Or "This will take too long." Or "Writing a book is hard."

All these statements and questions are nothing more than limiting beliefs.

They're made up ideas we cling to because they provide justification in our minds to not do it. Even though we know it will benefit us and our business.

Most of the time, these limiting beliefs are the result of over-complicating the process and the goals of Credibility Books.

It's tough for some people to grasp the concept of writing a short, value-based book that people will actually read.

They want to make it harder than it should be. I ask you now to trust the process and the results you've seen so far, and avoid this mistake at all costs.

Not providing value

The most important thing a Credibility Book can provide its readers is value. The book has to be extremely useful to them, whether it's walking them through a process step-by-step or giving them tips on how to make the most of your product or service.

What a Credibility Book should not be is an obvious promotional tool. People can see right through these salesy tactics, and when they do, they'll know right away that you're not trying to provide them with value but just trying to sell them something. While some of this can—and should—be included, try to limit the amount you talk about yourself, how great you are, and how wonderful your company is. That is not what a Credibility Book is for, and if you use it for that, you won't see the results you were hoping for from your book.

Not investing in your book

You've heard a lot about how Credibility Books don't take a lot of money to produce. And they don't—at least not in the same way that traditional books and publishing houses do. But there will still be some cost upfront. You need to be able to invest some money into getting your book written and created, and you'll need to be able to buy at least a few copies of your own book. Remember that you'll be using them down the line to convert prospects into customers.

While it's natural to be so excited about your Credibility Book that you overlook an issue like this, it's important to remember that anything of value is going to have at least a small price attached to it. The good news is that with Credibility Books, that cost is very low, so it's easier to prepare for.

Expecting to make a lot of money from book sales alone

Remember that your Credibility Book is definitely going to make you money down the line. But you shouldn't count on your Credibility Book making a ton of money on its own. Credibility Books aren't written so that they can be featured on best-seller lists and make a ton of money like a novel would. While you may make a few bucks off your book, it won't be enough to make up a supplementary income for your business. And if you expect it to, you'll likely be disappointed.

The value that Credibility Books bring may not come in the form of cash flowing into your business through the sale of books. The value comes in the positioning a Credibility Book gives you as the obvious, go-to expert in the marketplace. After all, your primary revenue source is your main product or service and not book sales.

Having a weak book cover

Many new authors don't invest the time they need in researching a great book cover. Yes, you need to research this. Meaning, reviewing other book covers that you like and find engaging. Ones that you can model. Ones that you can gain inspiration from. Too many authors simply turn the entire process over to a graphic designer and give them 100 percent control. Don't do this. Take the time necessary to visualize the right book cover for you, and then give a professional your ideas and then let them do their magic.

Waiting too long to get started

While no one should embark on writing a Credibility Book before they are ready, no one should wait to write a Credibility Book if they are ready to start reaping the benefits of having one. If you know you have the means to do it, have a great service, and know the exact value that you'll be providing to customers and prospects, and you need more customers, then now is the time to get started on your Credibility Book.

Waiting to get started will only mean delaying properly positioning yourself in the marketplace and waiting to establish yourself as the most credible and authoritative voice in the industry, and that means delaying increased profits. Why wait? Pull the trigger and get started now.

Doing it all yourself

Writing a book can be extremely daunting, even when you're self-publishing. You'll need to create graphics and content, and then get it distributed and promote it to those you want to read it. And of course, you'll still need to be running your business in the meanwhile. Business owners can do it themselves, but they shouldn't have to. Not when there is so much help out there. Don't go it alone. Find a professional who can help you plan, produce, publish, and promote your Credibility Book. Not only will you save time and effort, but you'll also be working with people who can ensure your Credibility Book is the huge success it deserves to be.

Ten Common Myths... Busted!

Hopefully we've already busted a lot of myths about Credibility Books. But believe it or not, there are still a few more we haven't touched on. There's no doubt you've thought at least of one or two of these myths. And now we're going to show you why these should never hold you back.

I don't know where to start.

Hopefully you've read this book to this point and have a much clearer picture of where to start.

The key success factor is to just get started in the first place.

And we can help with that.

In addition to this book, we also provide online training courses, coaching, and a bunch of other stuff to help guide you through your Credibility Book journey. We'll share more details about all of that at the end of this book.

I'm not a good enough writer.

You do not have to be a good writer. You're a business owner providing a product or service to your market. That's how you make your money. Every day you talk with customers and prospects answering their questions. A Credibility Book is an extension of you answering those questions. To write a powerful, engaging, and very valuable Credibility Book, all you have to do is write as you talk. Then with some minor editing, the book will move and flow as effortlessly as a mountain stream.

It takes a lot of time to write a book.

It doesn't have to. And that's the beauty of Credibility Books. They are short, sweet, and to-the-point.

You don't even have to write a word of it either.

For example, let's say you want to write an FAQ/SAQ style book. You can simply record yourself answering the questions on your cell phone and then get the recording transcribed. Of course, you will need to do some editing and polishing, but the actual writing will be done without you writing a word.

Many of our clients use our "Interview Style" book-writing process. This style is when one of our professionals interviews you and records the conversation. Our interviewer asks the questions, and you answer them. Then we get that transcribed and edited until it reads well. It's very effective because the interviewer will ask follow-up questions that probe even deeper, which makes the content that much more powerful.

I don't know what to write about.

I have done my absolute best to destroy that myth inside this book. All you have to do is go back and reread Parts Two and Three, and you should have a very clear picture of what to write about.

If you're still feeling unsure, I promise it is nothing more than a mental block you're having.

Let's be honest—you're here right now reading a Credibility Book. And I would bet that you've gotten a ton of value out of it.

My question to you is, don't you think you can do the same for your business? Of course you can.

This is a simple and proven process. Trust it.

I've never written a book before, and I don't know how.

Most of our customers and the people that read this book and contact us have never written a book before. If that's you, you're in good company.

In fact, it's better if you haven't written a book before.

Here's why.

You don't have all the "traditional publishing" garbage in your head clouding your judgment and preventing you from taking action.

To the people who have never written a book before, I say to you, "Great! Thank God! No go write your Credibility Book."

I'm on a tight budget and can't afford it.

Perfect. Often the people who need a Credibility Book the most are on a limited budget. That's why we use the process that we do and provide the support and tools that we do, to keep costs down but still create a world-class book that generates leads like crazy.

I don't know how to actually publish a book.

Hopefully by now you have a much better understanding of how to self-publish a book. And it shouldn't be as scary as you thought. In fact, it should be exhilarating to know you can publish a life-changing book of your own in just a few weeks. But again, you don't have to—and probably shouldn't—go it alone, and we also have additional resources for you at the end of this book.

I should just publish an ebook only.

No. I can't stress this enough. You need both an ebook and a print book. The print book will do most of your heavy lifting when it comes to lead generation. When using Amazon's KDP platform, you can do both at the same time. It just makes sense to have both.

The technology is too complicated.

This myth couldn't be further from the truth. Amazon KDP makes it super simple to publish your book. Sure, some things have a learning curve, but we'll be in your corner every step of the way to guide you through any areas you may have difficulty with.

Book cover design is hard and expensive.

This is another myth that drives me nuts. It's true that your cover is *very* important. Regardless of what people say, people do judge books by their cover. But that doesn't mean they have to be hard to design or expensive. Many services design book covers for next to nothing. And they're all very good too. You can do a simple Google search and come up with more than enough options. But don't worry, we help all out clients in this area as well.

BONUS: What if I want more help?

That's what we do.

We have an online training course, tools, templates, and even pre-written Credibility Books in tons of industries and topics.

We're here to help. You can find out all the details at the end of this book.

What Success Looks Like—A Case Study

Greg's Case Study is one that truly shows the power of what a Credibility Book can do for one's business.

Greg and I go back aways. We lost touch for a while but began meeting again when he started his consulting company. That's when I first introduced him to Credibility Books.

It didn't take Greg long to buy in. And after a few consultations and trainings and some guidance from me, he published his first book. And just like most Credibility Books, it was not traditional.

His first book was a recap of a seminar he attended. He wanted to write several blog posts about what he learned and how it may help his clients. But instead of twelve blog posts, he wrote a Credibility Book—or a "booklet" as he likes to call them.

Once that first book was complete, he realized he had a framework he could use over and over to create similar books. That's how *Amalgamate* was born. This new framework made creating his second book super easy and fast.

He now hands out one of his *Amalgamate* books to every new person he meets and always gets a thank you a week or so later.

To this point, he has given out three hundred books, which has directly resulted in over $30k in new business!

Even though one book is enough, due to his success, Greg has published four *Amalgamate* books.

His publishing success has also led to him publishing a book with a more traditional publisher.

The growth and success of his consulting company is directly related to Greg publishing that first Credibility Book.

Do This Now

If I have done my job, you now know the solution to the problems you're having when it comes to gaining more credibility and authority in your marketplace. You now know that publishing a Credibility Book is a surefire way to get the authority you're looking for. And you also know that it will be much more effective than writing a traditional book and going through a traditional publishing house to do it.

That's all great, but how do you do it? How do you get that book you've been wanting to write for so long but have been so reluctant to try?

That's where we come in. Earlier in this book, we talked about how having a professional on your side is a great way to get the guidance you need to ensure you get the best results possible in the least amount of time.

So, what can we do for you?

We will work with you to get the most powerful Credibility Book in your hands in six weeks or less.

But when the six weeks is up, we don't just leave you hanging there with a printed book you have no idea what to do with. We'll also help you promote it and get it out there, so your prospects and customers know about it, get it, and read it.

All of this will point back to the one main solution: getting you recognized as the authority and expert in your industry, building you the credibility you need to be more successful and get those profits rolling in through the door.

That brings us here. Your next steps.

It basically comes down to two options. You need to pick the best one for you.

Option 1 – Do-it-Yourself: Take what you've learned in this book and publish your own Credibility Book. This is a longer and tougher road, because you need to do it all yourself. And you'll certainly hit some roadblocks that will slow your progress. But if you're willing to go the DIY route, go for it. You have our blessing, and our book full of tips.

Option 2 – Done-With-You: You can work with us directly and get your own Credibility Book published in as little as six weeks. We cover every single aspect of the writing and publishing process, so no stone is left unturned. And the best part? We do it live with you so you can ask questions and make sure you're always on the right track. If this sounds like a good option for you, I invite you to take the first step, which is to contact us at the webpage below:

https://CredibilityBook.com/talk

Attend Our Free Webclass

For the people who want even more information on publishing their own Credibility Book, we have created an online webclass.

On this webclass you'll discover:

- ✓ What the #1 purpose of your book should be (Hint: it's not book sales!)
- ✓ Why traditional publishing is the worst time and money trap ever and how to harness the power of a short, concise book that people actually want to read
- ✓ The four-step publishing model that's turning our clients from total unknowns into powerful authorities in six weeks or less
- ✓ A simple four-part framework that will show you exactly what to include in your book, allowing you to write it effortlessly and quickly
- ✓ The secrets of cover design so your book will look great, get attention, and make people want to read it
- ✓ How to use your new book to generate tons of leads and customers—and do most of it on autopilot
- ✓ Plus much more!

To attend the webclass, go here now:

https://CredibilityBook.com/webclass

Before You Leave a Review

Thank you again for investing in and reading this book. If you got this far you deserve to be congratulated!

I truly hope that by reading this book you now understand the power in having a Credibility Book for your business.

As a future author, you will soon realize that us authors live and die by the reviews we receive from our readers. If you liked this book, I'd really appreciate it if you left a 5-star review on Amazon.

If for some reason this book did not meet your expectations then before you leave a not-so-good review, please contact me at the link below and let me know what you would like me to improve. The beauty of publishing online is that I can instantly add content, fix errors and update information.

I sincerely want you to be 100% satisfied with this book so please contact me if you have any questions:

https://CredibilityBook.com/contact

To leave a 5-Start Review go to:

https://CredibilityBook.com/review

www.ingramcontent.com/pod-product-compliance
Lightning Source LLC
Chambersburg PA
CBHW070449220526
45466CB00004B/1790